WITHDRAWN

JUNIOR COLLEGE DISTRICT
of St. Louis - St. Louis County
LIBRARY

7508 Forsyth Blvd.
St. Louis, Missouri 63105

bd   PRINTED IN U S A

D1288431

ERWIN PANOFSKY

RENAISSANCE AND RENASCENCES

IN WESTERN ART

• FIGURA •

10

STUDIES EDITED BY

THE INSTITUTE OF ART HISTORY

UNIVERSITY OF UPPSALA

also published as

THE GOTTESMAN LECTURES

UPPSALA UNIVERSITY

VII

RENAISSANCE
AND RENASCENCES
IN WESTERN ART

By ERWIN PANOFSKY

PLATES

ALMQVIST & WIKSELL · STOCKHOLM

© *Almqvist & Wiksell | Gebers Förlag AB*, STOCKHOLM

Distributed in Continental Europe,
and the Near East by
RUSSAK & COMPANY LTD.,
Rosenvængets Allé 22, Copenhagen, Denmark,
by special arrangement with
ALMQVIST & WIKSELL, Stockholm

PRINTED IN SWEDEN BY

Almqvist & Wiksells

BOKTRYCKERI AKTIEBOLAG

UPPSALA 1960

FIG. 1. Rome, The Pantheon.

FIG. 2. Trèves, Our Lady's Church.

FIG. 3. Palladio, Villa Capra (known as "Villa Rotonda"), near Vicenza.

FIG. 4. Leone Battista Alberti, Mantua, S. Andrea, interior.

FIG. 5. Nuremberg, S. Sebaldus, interior of the choir.

FIG. 6. Fiesole, Badia, façade.

FIG. 7. Filippo Brunelleschi, Florence, Pazzi Chapel, façade.

FIG. 8. Lorsch, the Carolingian "Torhalle".

FIG. 9. Paris, Bibliothèque Nationale, MS. lat. 12108 (St. Augustine, *Quaestiones in Heptateuchon*, middle of the eighth century), fol. C v., display page.

FIG. 10. Autun, Bibliothèque Municipale, MS. 3 (Gundohinus Gospels, completed 754), fol. 187 v., St. Luke.

FIG. 11. Vienna, Schatzkammer, So-called "Gospels of Charlemagne", fol. *76 v.*, St. Mark (somewhat enlarged).

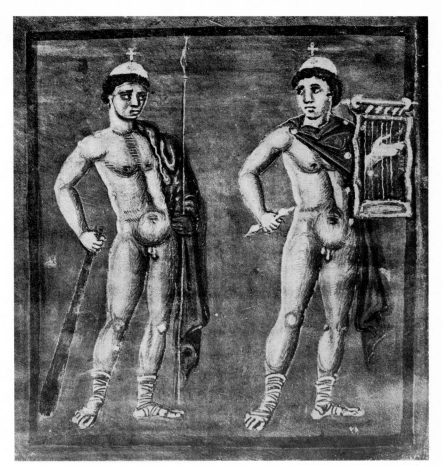

FIG. 12. Leiden, University Library, Cod. Voss. lat. 79 (*Aratea*, first half of ninth century) fol. 16 v., The Twins.

FIG. 13. Utrecht, University Library, MS. 484 ("Utrecht Psalter", 820–830), fol. 6 v., illustration of Psalm XI (XII).

FIG. 14. Utrecht, same manuscript, fol. 59 v.,
Lions, detail (enlarged) of illustration of
Psalm CIII (CIV).

FIG. 15. Utrecht, same manuscript, fol. 14 v.,
Classical Aqueduct, detail (enlarged) of illustration of Psalm XXV (XXVI).

FIG. 16. Utrecht, same manuscript, fol. 57, Atlas, detail (enlarged) of illustration of Psalm XCVIII (XCIX).

FIG. 17. Rome, Vatican Library, Cod. Barb. lat. 2154 (Renaissance copy after a Carolingian manuscript of the *Chronograph of 354*), fol. 8, Saturn. — FIG. 18. Rome, same manuscript as Fig. 17, fol. 9, Mars.

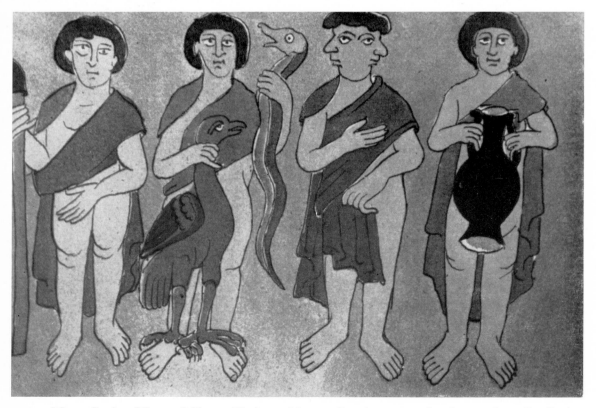

FIG. 19. Monte Cassino, Library, MS. 132 (Hrabanus Maurus, *De universo*, copy, dated 1023, after a Carolingian manuscript), p. 386, Saturn, Jupiter, Janus, Neptune.

FIG. 20. Munich, Staatsbibliothek, The Crucifixion, Carolingian ivory.

FIG. 21. Arles, St.-Trophîme, façade,
middle of the twelfth century.

FIG. 22. Bari, Cathedral, Throne of
1098, detail.

FIG. 23. Berlin, Kaiser Friedrich Museum, Entry into Jerusalem, Byzantine ivory of the tenth century, detail (enlarged).

FIG. 24. Lisieux, Cathedral, Sarcophagus, probably of Bishop Arnulf (reigned 1141–1181).

FIG. 26. Lyons, Musée Municipal, Juggler (from Bourges), third quarter of the twelfth century.

FIG. 25. Reims, Cathedral, Profile Head, interior of west façade, middle of the thirteenth century.

FIG. 27. Bordeaux, Musée Lapidaire, Gallo-Roman Entablature.

FIG. 28. St.-Gilles, Abbey Church, Detail of Entablature, *ca.* 1140.

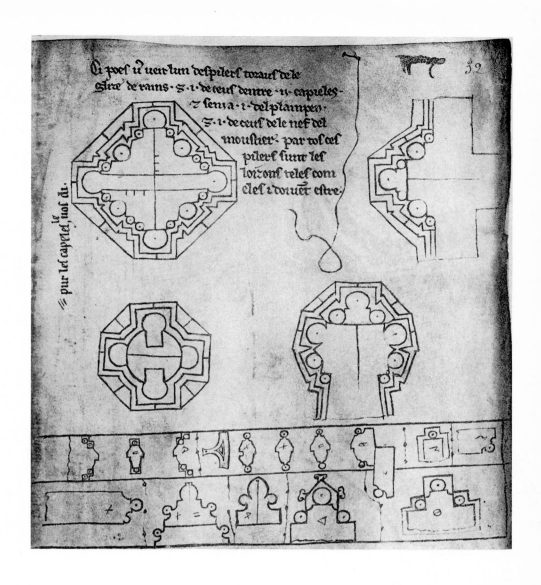

FIG. 29. Villard de Honnecourt, Cross Sections of Piers and Moldings in Reims Cathedral, Paris, Bibliothèque Nationale, MS. fr. 19093 ("Album", *ca.* 1235), fol. 32.

FIG. 30. St.-Gilles, Abbey Church, Sts. John the Evangelist and Peter, *ca.* 1140.

FIG. 31. Master Gilabertus, St. Andrew (from St.-Etienne), Toulouse, Musée Lapidaire, probably towards 1130.

FIG. 32. Chartres, Cathedral, west façade (central portal), Kings and Queens of Israel (and, by implication, France), toward 1145.

FIG. 33. Chartres, Cathedral, north transept (left portal), The Annunciation, *ca.* 1215.

FIG. 34. Naumburg, Cathedral, jubé, Last Supper, *ca.* 1260.

FIG. 35. Reims, Cathedral, north transept (left portal), St. Peter, 1220–1225.

FIG. 36. Rome, Museo Nazionale, Bust of Antoninus Pius.

FIG. 37. Reims, Cathedral, north transept (left portal), The Ressurrected, 1220–1225.

FIG. 38. Reims, Cathedral, Capital, 1220–1225.

FIG. 39. Reims, Musée Lapidaire, So-called "Sarcophagus of Jovinus", detail.

FIG. 40. Reims, Cathedral, west façade (central portal), The Annunciation and The Visitation, *ca.* 1230.

FIG. 43. New York, Metropolitan Museum, Tanagra figurine (No. 06.1114).

FIG. 41. Freiburg i. Br., Kunstgeschichtliches Institut, *Mater dolorosa*, French bronze statuette, *ca.* 1200.

FIG. 42. Vienna, Kunsthistorisches Museum, Juno, Greek bronze statuette.

FIG. 44. Paris, Juritzky Collection, Hercules (prefiguring Christ) Killing the Lion, cameo, probably second quarter of the thirteenth century (plaster cast, enlarged, photograph supplied by Prof. H. Wentzel).

FIG. 45. London, British Museum, Embarkation of Noah, cameo, probably middle of the thirteenth century (plaster cast, enlarged, photograph supplied by Prof. H. Wentzel).

FIG. 47. Pisa, Camposanto, Dionysus Vase, detail.

FIG. 46. Nicolo Pisano, Presentation of Christ (detail),
Pisa, Pulpit in the Baptistry, *ca.* 1260.

FIG. 48. Nicolo Pisano, Fortitude in the Guise of Hercules, Pisa, Pulpit in the Baptistry, *ca.* 1260.

FIG. 49. Lyons, Bibliothèque Municipale, MS. 742 (*Ovide moralisé* in verse, third quarter of the fourteenth century), fol. 4, Creation of the World and Animation of Man by Prometheus.

FIG. 50. Lyons, same manuscript as Fig. 49, fol. 87, Minerva, the Muses and the Pierids on Mount Helicon (enlarged).

FIG. 51. Paris, Bibliothèque Nationale, MS. fr. 871 (*Ovide moralisé* in verse, *ca.* 1400), fol. 116, Apollo, Minerva, Pegasus, the Muses, and the Pierids on Mount Helicon.

FIG. 52. Paris, same manuscript as Fig. 51, fol. 149 v., Orpheus Charming the Animals.

FIG. 53. Munich, Staatsbibliothek, clm. 14271 (Remigius of Auxerre, *Commentary on Martianus Capella, ca.* 1100), fol. 11 v., The Pagan Gods.

FIG. 54. Paris, Bibliothèque Nationale, MS. lat. 15158 (Ovid, *De remediis amoris*, forming part of a *Psychomachia* manuscript, dated 1289), fol. 47, The Story of Pyramus and Thisbe.

FIG. 55. Oxford, Bodleian Library, MS. Douce 195 (*Roman de la Rose*, ca. 1470), fol. 150, Pygmalion Dressing His Statue (enlarged).

FIG. 56. Paris, Bibliothèque Nationale, MS. fr. 373 (*Ovide moralisé* in verse, towards 1380), fol. 207, Venus with the Sea Goose (enlarged).

FIG. 57. Geneva, Bibliothèque Publique et Universitaire, MS. fr. 176 (*Ovide moralisé* in verse, end of the fourteenth century), fol. 216, Venus with the Sea Goose, improved version (enlarged).

FIG. 58. Copenhagen, Royal Library, MS. Thott 399, 2° (*Ovide moralisé* in verse, preceded by a French translation of the Introduction to Petrus Berchorius' *Ovidius moralizatus*, towards 1480), fol. 9 v., Venus with the Flower-adorned Slate (enlarged).

FIG. 59. Schöngrabern (Austria), Church, Sisyphus, Tantalus and Ixion, *ca.* 1230.

FIG. 60. Dresden, Landesbibliothek, *Sachsenspiegel* (fourteenth century replica of an earlier model), fol. 68 v., Legal Scene.

FIG. 61. Auxerre, Cathedral, west façade, Hercules; Joseph Cast into the Pit (Genesis, XXXVII), *ca.* 1280.

FIG. 62. Auxerre, Cathedral, west façade, Satyr; The Dream of Pharaoh (Genesis, XLI), *ca.* 1280.

Etabstulit sicut oues populum suum ./
&pduxit eos taquam gregem indeserto

Eteduxit eos inspe &nontimuerunt ./

FIG. 63. Stuttgart, Würtembergische Landesbibliothek, MS. Biblia Folio 23 (Stuttgart Psalter, early ninth century), fol. 93 v., Illustrations (slightly enlarged) of Psalm LXXVII (LXXVIII).

FIG. 64. Auxerre, Cathedral, west façade, *Amor carnalis*, *ca.* 1280.

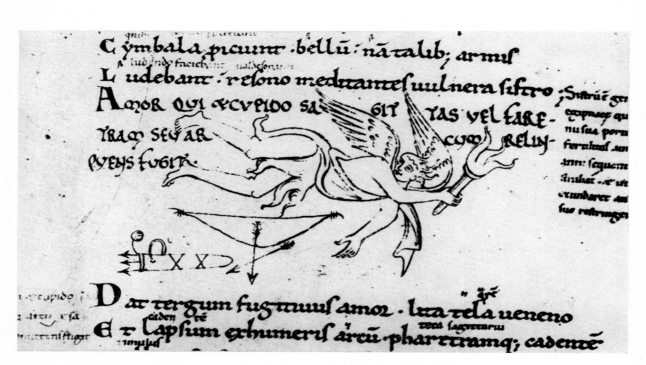

FIG. 65. Lyons, Bibliothèque du Palais des Arts, MS. 22 (Prudentius, *Psychomachia*, about 1100), fol. 17 v., Cupid in Flight (slightly enlarged).

FIG. 66. Master Wiligelmus, Cupid with Inverted Torch, Modena, Cathedral, west façade, *ca.* 1170.

FIG. 67. Master Wiligelmus, Cupid with Inverted Torch and Ibis, Modena, Cathedral, west façade, *ca.* 1170.

FIG. 68. Osnabrück, Town Hall, Chalice known as the *Kaiserpokal*, towards 1300 (photographs reproduced in Figs. 68–74 supplied by Prof. H. Wentzel).

FIGS. 69–71. Osnabrück, same object, details from *cuppa*. Virtues and Vices.

FIG. 69.

F<small>IG</small>. 70.

F<small>IG</small>. 71.

FIG. 72. Osnabrück, same object as Fig. 68, cover.

FIG. 73. Osnabrück, same object as Fig. 68, cover, detail. — FIG. 74. Formerly Paris, Roger Collection, *Hercules Musarum*, classical cameo (plaster cast, enlarged).

FIG. 75.

FIG. 76.

FIGS. 75–77. Osnabrück, same object as Fig. 68, cover, details.

FIG. 77.

FIG. 78. Monreale, Cathedral, Cloister, "Mithras" Capital, between 1172 and 1189.

FIG. 79. Mithras Killing the Bull, Rome, Museo Capitolino.

FIG. 80. Mithras Twisting the Horns of the Bull, woodcut from Vincenzo Cartari, *Imagini dei Dei degli antichi*, Venice, 1674, p. 34.

FIG. 81. Mithras Killing the Bull, woodcut from the same publication as Fig. 80, p. 275.

FIG. 82. Vézelay, Ste.-Madeleine (central portal), detail of lintel, Sacrifice of a Bull, between 1120 and 1132.

FIG. 83. Charlieu, St.-Fortunat, small portal, Wedding of Cana and Sacrifice of Animals, middle of the twelfth century.

FIG. 85. Mantua, Broletto, Statue of Virgil, probably about 1227.

FIG. 84. Benedetto Antelami (?), Statue of Virgil, Mantua, Palazzo Ducale, *ca.* 1215.

FIG. 86. Mantuan *grosso* of 1257 (enlarged).

P. VERGILII
MARONIS A
AETERNAE
SVI MEMORI
AE IMAGO

FIG. 87. Andrea Mantegna (after),
Project for the Statue of Virgil
Planned in 1499, Paris, Louvre.

FIG. 88. Paris, Bibliothèque de l'Arsenal, MS. 1036 (Sūfi, *Liber de locis stellarum*, middle of the thirteenth century), fol. 22 v., Gemini.

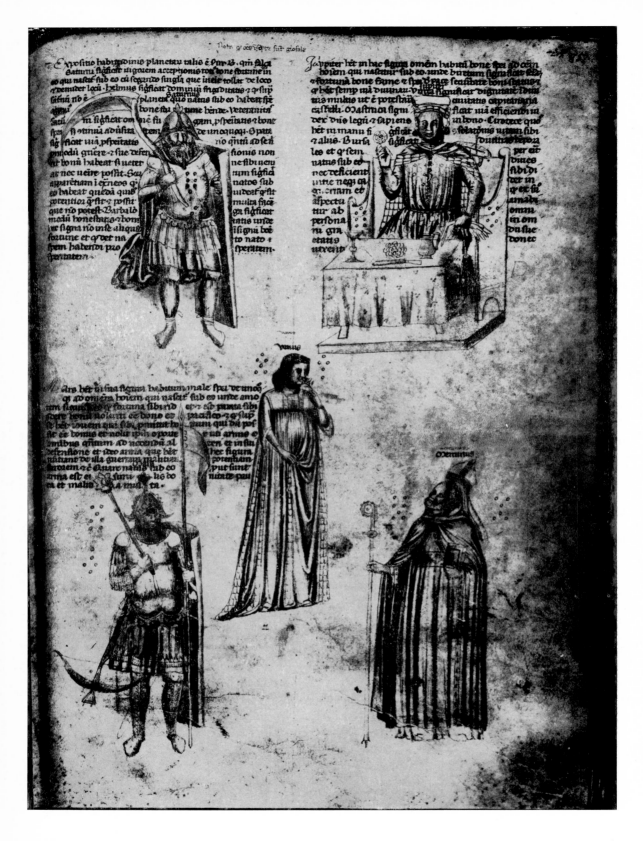

FIG. 89. Munich, Staatsbibliothek, clm. 10268 (Michael Scotus, *Liber introductorius*, second half of the fourteenth century), fol. 85, Saturn, Jupiter, Mars, Venus, Mercury.

FIG. 90. New York, Pierpont Morgan Library, MS. 785 (Abū Ma'šar, *Liber astrologiae*, fraudulently claimed by Georgius Zothori Zapari Fenduli, towards 1403), fol. 48, Mercury in Exaltation.

FIG. 91. Giotto, Crucifixion, Padua, Arena Chapel, *ca.* 1305.

FIG. 92. Duccio di Buoninsegna, Crucifixion, Siena, Opera del Duomo, 1308–1311.

FIG. 93. Giotto, Lamentation of Christ, Padua, Arena Chapel, *ca.* 1305.

FIG. 94. London, British Museum, MS. Add. 10546 (Bible of Moutier-Grandval, second half of the ninth century), fol. 25 v., Moses Displaying the Tables of the Law.

FIG. 95. Villard de Honnecourt, Choir Chapel of Reims Cathedral, inside view, Paris, Bibliothèque Nationale, same manuscript as Fig. 29, fol. 30 v.

FIG. 96. Villard de Honnecourt, Choir Chapel of Reims Cathedral, outside view, same manuscript as Fig. 29, fol. 31.

FIG. 97. Florence, Baptistry, Dream of Pharaoh, mosaic (much restored), first half of the thirteenth century.

FIG. 98. Monreale, Cathedral, Last Supper, mosaic, late twelfth century.

FIG. 99. Duccio di Buoninsegna, Last Supper, Siena, Opera del Duomo, 1308–1311.

FIG. 100. Taddeo Gaddi, Rejection of Joachim's Offering and Presentation of the Virgin, Florence, S. Croce (Baroncelli Chapel), probably fourth decade of the fourteenth century.

FIG. 101. Ambrogio Lorenzetti, *Presentation of Christ*, Florence, Uffizi, dated 1342.

FIG. 102. Maître des Heures du Maréchal de Boucicaut (workshop), Presentation of Christ, Paris, Bibliothèque Nationale, MS. lat. 10538 (Book of Hours *ca.* 1415), fol. 78.

FIG. 103. Pietro Lorenzetti, Birth of the Virgin, Siena, Opera del Duomo, dated 1342.

FIG. 104. Ambrogio Lorenzetti, Annunciation, Siena, Accademia, dated 1344.

FIG. 105. Pietro Lorenzetti (workshop), Last Supper, Assisi, S. Francesco (lower church), between 1320–1330.

FIG. 106. Niccolo Pisano, Pisa, Pulpit in the Baptistry, *ca.* 1260.

FIG. 107. Giotto, Birth of the Virgin, Padua, Arena Chapel (detail), *ca.* 1305.

FIG. 108. Pietro Lorenzetti (workshop), Flaggellation of Christ (detail), Assisi, S. Francesco (lower church), 1320–1330

FIG. 109. Francesco Traini, Triumph of Death, Pisa, Camposanto, *ca.* 1350.

SEP· DNI· GALLI· AGRELLI· IVDICIS· OPARII· OPE· SCE· MARIE·

FIG. 110. Pisa, Camposanto, Roman Sarcophagus (reused for the burial of Gallo Agnello).

FIG. 111. Florence, Cathedral, Porta della Mandorla, embrasure, Prudence, 1391–1396.

FIG. 112. Ambrogio Lorenzetti, Martyrdom of the Franciscans in Morocco (detail showing Minerva, Mars and Venus), Siena, S. Francesco, *ca.* 1330.

FIG. 113. Giotto, Banquet of Herod, Florence, S. Croce (Peruzzi Chapel), *ca.* 1330.

FIG. 114. Giotto, Allegory of Justice (detail showing *remuneratio*), Padua, Arena Chapel, *ca.* 1305.

FIG. 115. Formerly Florence, R. di Montalvo Collection, Meleager Sarcophagus, detail.

FIG. 116. Darmstadt, Landesbibliothek, Cod. 101 (Italian translation of Petrarch's *De viris illustribus*, ca. 1400), fol. 19, Siege of a City by Alexander the Great.

FIG. 117. Rome, S. Nicola in Carcere.

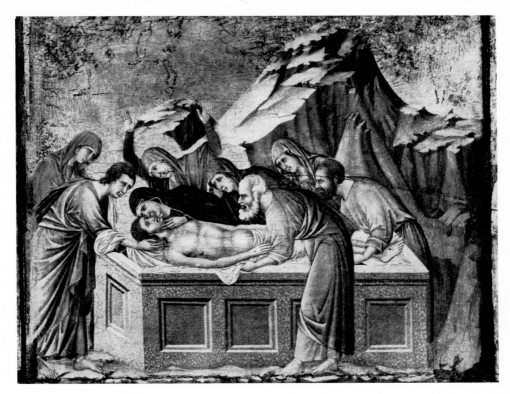

FIG. 118. Duccio di Buoninsegna, Lamentation of Christ, Siena, Opera del Duomo, 1308–1311.

FIG. 119. Jean Pucelle, Lamentation of Christ, New York, Metropolitan Museum (Cloisters), Hours of Jeanne d'Evreux, fol. 82 v., 1325–1328.

FIG. 120. Duccio di Buoninsegna, Annunciation of the Virgin's Death, Siena, Opera del Duomo, 1308–1311.

FIG. 121. Jean Pucelle, Annunciation, same manuscript as Fig. 119, fol. 16.

FIG. 122. Jean Bondol (?), Four Infancy Scenes, The Hague, Museum Meermano-Westreenianum, MS. 10.B.23 (Bible Historiale of Charles V, dated 1371), fol. 467.

FIG. 123. Jean Bondol, Portrait of Charles V, same manuscript as Fig. 122, fol. 2.

FIG. 124. Jacquemart de Hesdin (?), Flight into Egypt, Brussels, Bibliothèque Royale, MS. 11060/61 (Book of Hours of the Duc de Berry, before 1402), fol. 106.

FIG. 125. The Limbourg Brothers, Presentation of Christ, Chantilly, Musée Condé (*Très Riches Heures du Duc de Berry*, 1413–1416), fol. *54 v.*

FIG. 126. Maître des Heures du Maréchal de Bouiccaut, King Charles VI in Conversation with Pierre Salmon, Geneva, Bibliothèque Publique et Universitaire, MS. fr. 165 (*Dialogues de Pierre Salmon*, 1411–1412), fol. 4 (slightly enlarged).

FIG. 127. Maître des Heures du Maréchal de Boucicaut, Annunciation to the Shepherds, Paris, Musée Jacquemart-André (Hours of the Maréchal de Boucicaut, this page *ca.* 1410), fol. 79 v.

FIG. 128. North Italian Master, Adoration of the Magi, *ca.* 1410, New York, Messrs. Rosenberg & Stiebel.

FIG. 129. Masaccio, The Trinity, Florence, S. M. Novella, probably between 1425 and 1427.

FIG. 130. Masaccio, Madonna, London, National Gallery, 1426 (reproduced by courtesy of the Trustees, the National Gallery, London).

FIG. 131. Donatello, So-called "Atys-Amorino" (more correctly: "Time as a Playful Child Throwing Dice"), Florence, Museo Nazionale, *ca.* 1440.

FIG. 131 a. Donatello, So-called "Atys-Amorino", rear view.

FIG. 132. Donatello, The Heart of the Miser, Padua, S. Antonio, towards 1450.

FIG. 133. Apollonio di Giovanni, Scene from the *Aeneid* (cassone front, detail), New Haven (Conn.), Yale University Art Gallery, *ca.* 1460 (reproduced by courtesy of the Yale University Art Gallery).

FIG. 134. Andrea del Castagno, David, Washington, D. C., National Gallery of Art, towards 1455 (reproduced by courtesy of the National Gallery of Art, Widener Collection).

FIG. 135. Andrea Mantegna, The Condemnation of St. James, Padua, Eremitani Church (destroyed), towards 1455.

FIG. 136. Florentine Master, Abduction of Helen (pen drawing in the "Florentine Picture Chronicle", *ca.* 1460), London, British Museum.

FIG. 137. Antonio Pollaiuolo, Hercules Fighting the Hydra, Florence, Uffizi, probably 1465–1470.

FIG. 138. Piero di Cosimo, The Finding of Vulcan, Hartford (Conn.), Wadsworth Atheneum, *ca.* 1485–1490.

FIG. 139. Piero di Cosimo, Vulcan, Assisted by Aeolus, as Teacher of Mankind, Ottawa, National Gallery, *ca.* 1485–1490 (reproduced by courtesy of the National Gallery, Ottawa).

FIG. 140. Piero di Cosimo, detail of Fig. 139.

FIG. 141. Piero di Cosimo, The Discovery of Honey, Worcester (Mass.), Worcester Art Museum, *ca.* 1498.

FIG. 142.

FIG. 142 a.

FIG. 142. Piero di Cosimo, details from Fig. 141.

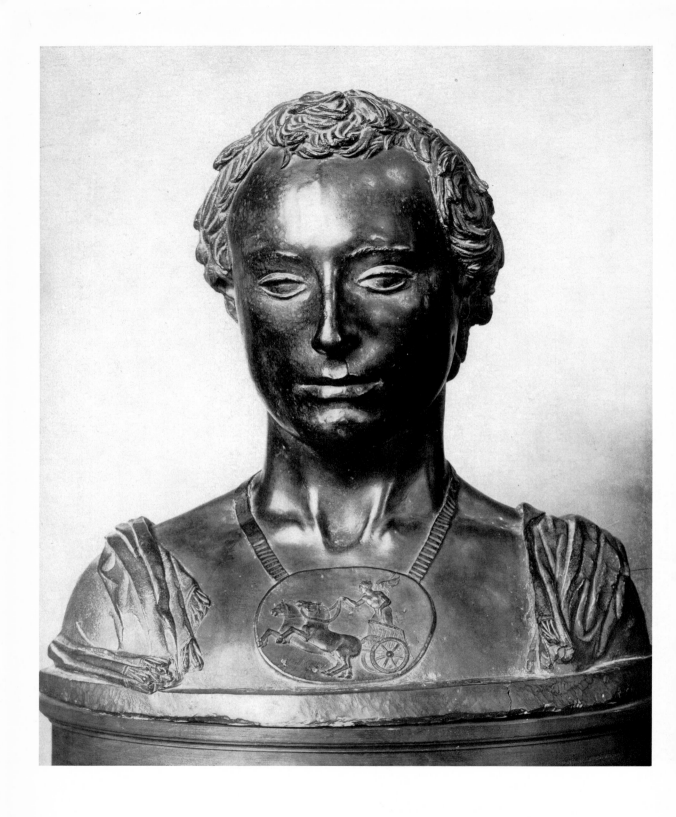

FIG. 143. Florentine Master, Bust of a Young Man (ascribed by some to Donatello), Florence, Museo Nazionale, probably 1470–1475.

FIG. 144. Maerten van Heemskerck, St. Luke Portraying the Virgin, Haarlem, Frans Hals Museum, dated 1532.

FIG. 145. Lucas Cranach the Elder, Cupid Unblindfolding Himself, Philadelphia, Pennsylvania Museum of Art, *ca.* 1525–1530.

FIG. 146. Nicolas Béatrizet after Baccio Bandinelli, The Combat of Lust and Reason, Engraving B. 44, dated 1545.

FIG. 147. Sandro Botticelli, The Birth of Venus, Florence, Uffizi, *ca.* 1480.

FIG. 148. Sandro Botticelli, The Realm of Venus ("*La Primavera*"), Florence, Uffizi, towards 1478.

FIG. 149. Sandro Botticelli, The Calumny of Apelles, Florence, Uffizi, *ca.* 1485.

FIG. 150. Filippino Lippi, Erato ("Allegory of Music"), Berlin, Kaiser Friedrich Museum, *ca.* 1500.

FIG. 151. Lysippus (after), Cupid Stringing His Bow, Rome, Museo Capitolino.

FIG. 152. Marcantonio Raimondi, Parnassus (after Raphael), Engraving B. 247.

FIG. 153. Raphael, Parnassus (detail), Rome, Vatican, 1509–1511.

FIG. 154. Raphael, School of Athens, Rome, Vatican 1509–1511.

FIG. 155. Titian, Feast of Venus (detail), Madrid, Prado.

FIG. 156. Rome, Biblioteca Vaticana, Cod. Pal. lat. 1370 (miscellaneous astrological treatises written in Germany about the middle of the fifteenth century), fol. 97 v., Mars (enlarged).

FIG. 157. Rome, Biblioteca Vaticana, Cod, Pal. lat. 291 (Hrabanus Maurus, *De universo*, German copy, datable in the first half of the fifteenth century, after a Carolingian manuscript), Saturn, Jupiter, Janus, Neptune.

325